BEGINNING PIANO SOLO

GREATEST POP HITS

ISBN 0-634-06826-1

7777 W. BLUEMOUND RD. P.O. BOX 13819 MILWAUKEE, WI 53213

Visit Hal Leonard Online at
www.halleonard.com

GREATEST POP HITS

CONTENTS

4   **Angel**
SARAH McLACHLAN

10   **Endless Love**
DIANA ROSS & LIONEL RICHIE

14   **Every Breath You Take**
THE POLICE

18   **Imagine**
JOHN LENNON AND THE PLASTIC ONO BAND

22   **Just the Way You Are**
BILLY JOEL

30   **Love Me Tender**
ELVIS PRESLEY

32   **Tears in Heaven**
ERIC CLAPTON

27   **Yesterday**
THE BEATLES

ANGEL

Words and Music by
SARAH McLACHLAN

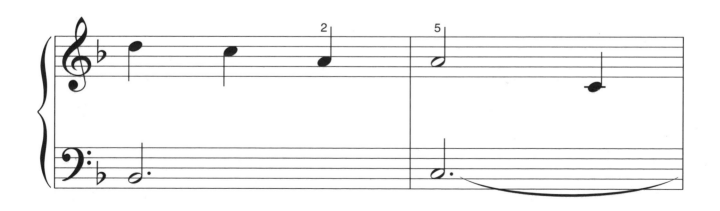

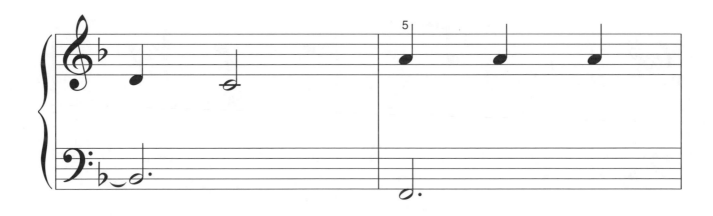

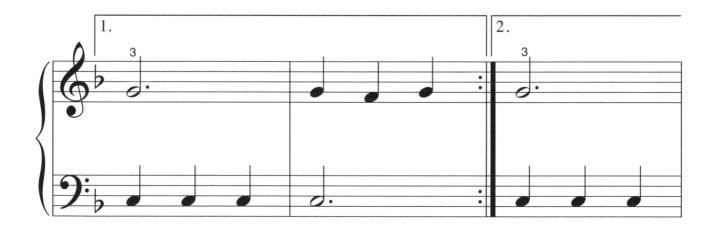

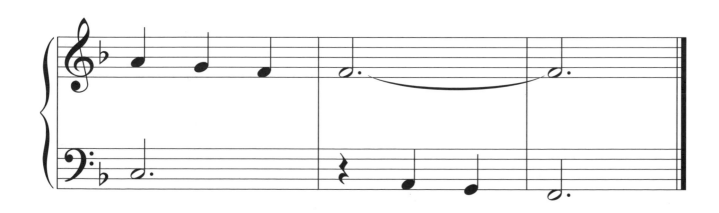

ENDLESS LOVE

Words and Music by
LIONEL RICHIE

Slowly

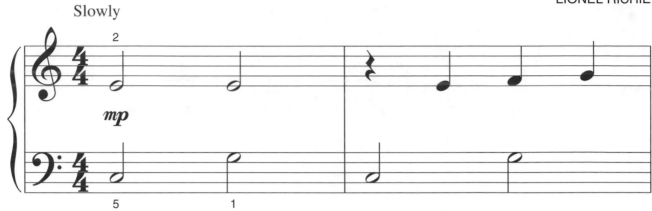

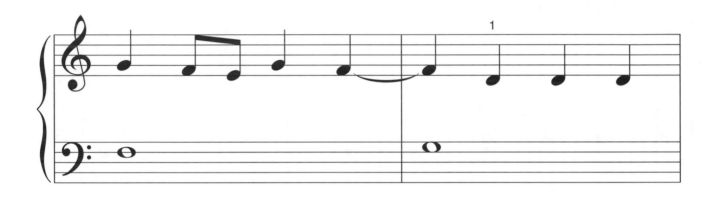

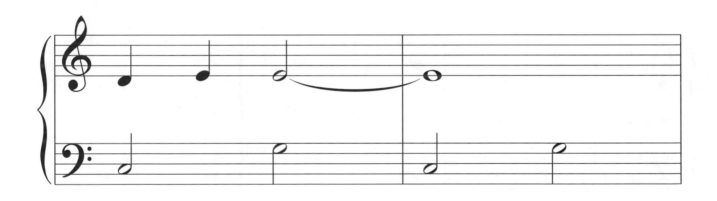

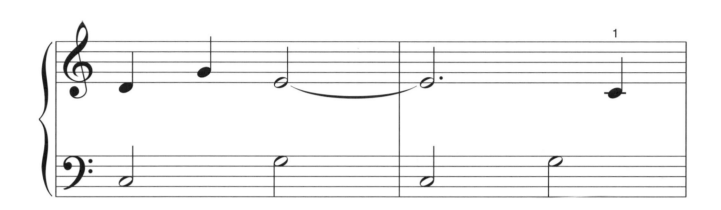

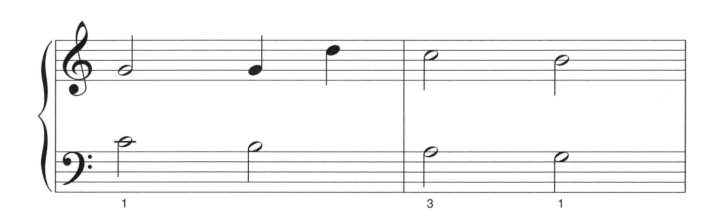

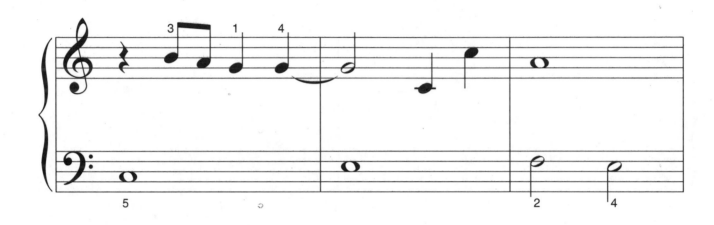

14 EVERY BREATH YOU TAKE

Music and Lyrics by
STING

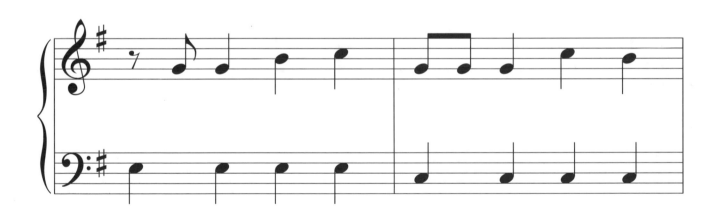

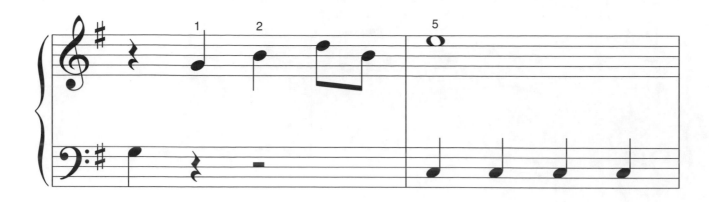

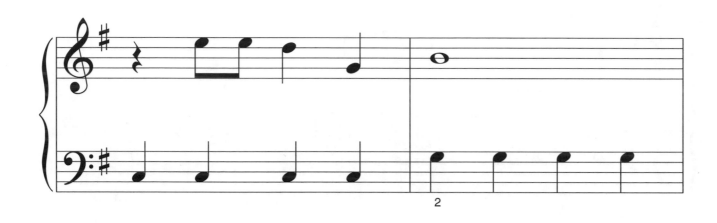

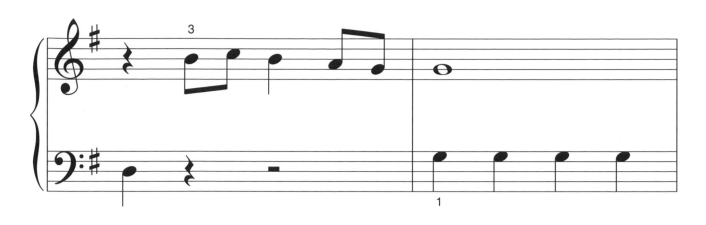

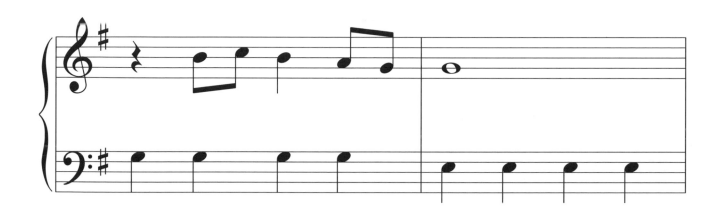

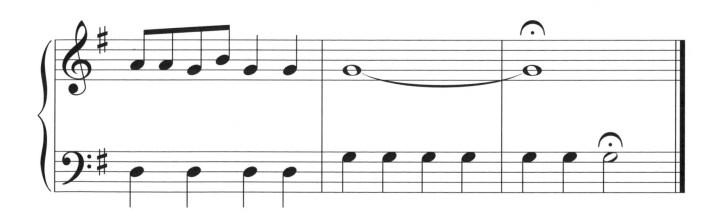

IMAGINE

Words and Music by
JOHN LENNON

Slowly

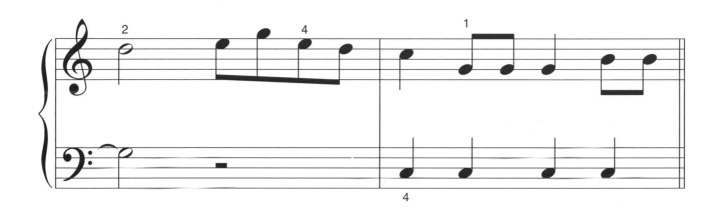

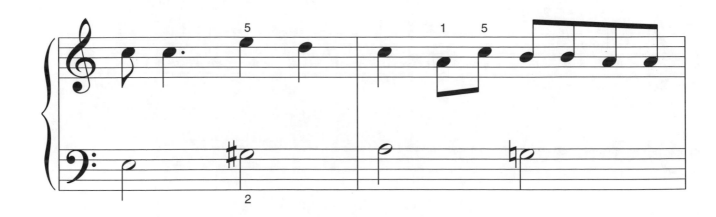

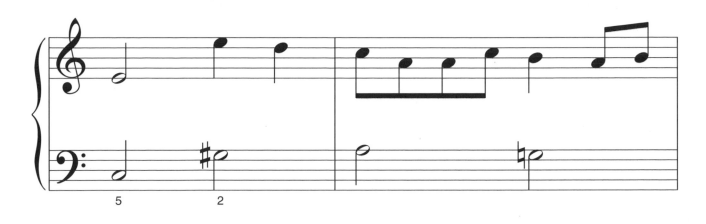

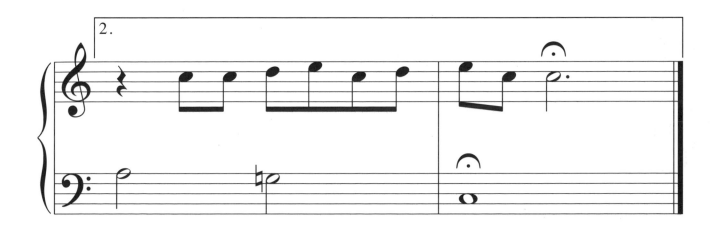

JUST THE WAY YOU ARE

Words and Music by
BILLY JOEL

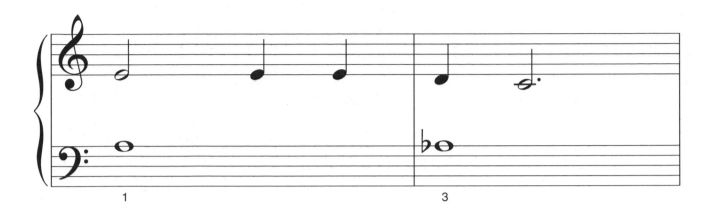

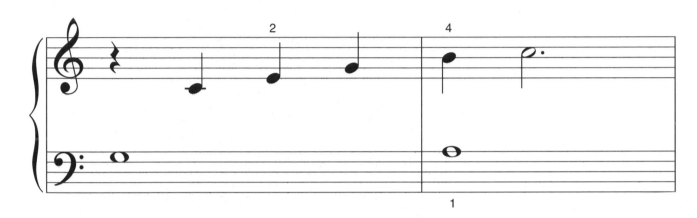

To Coda ⊕

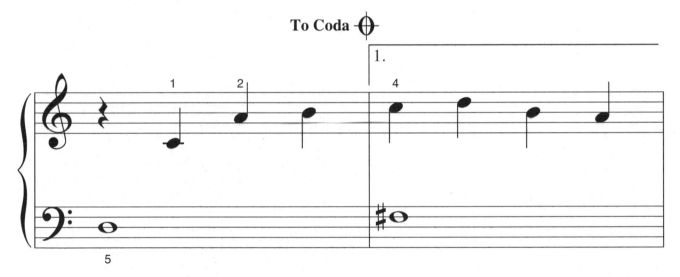

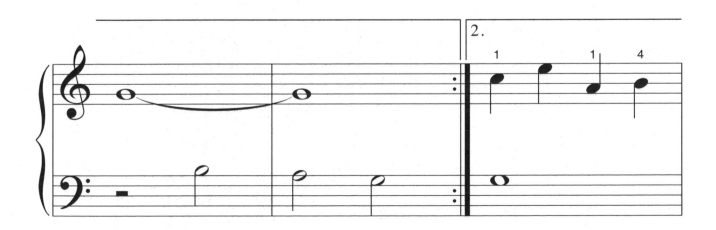

23

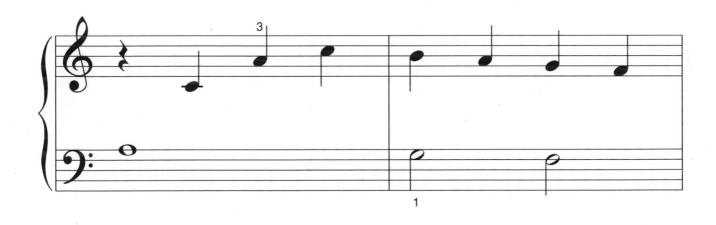

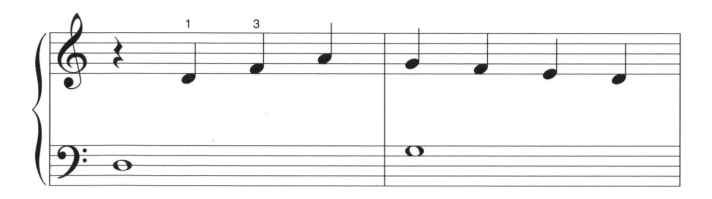

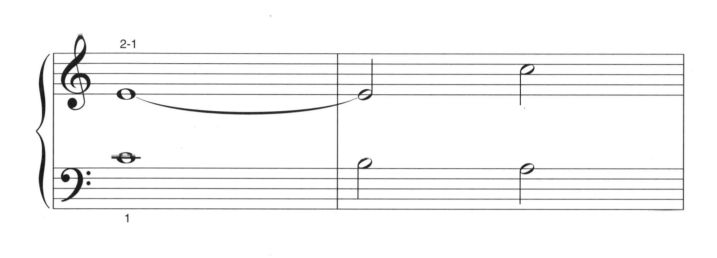

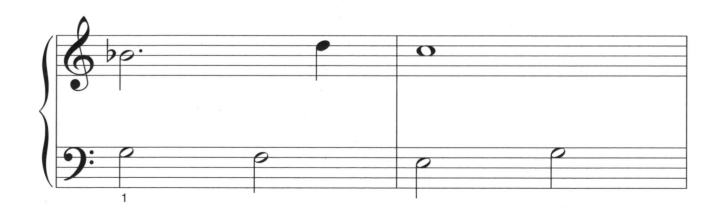

D.C. al Coda

CODA

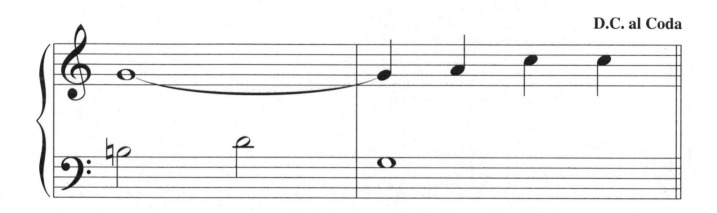

Yesterday

Words and Music by JOHN LENNON
and PAUL McCARTNEY

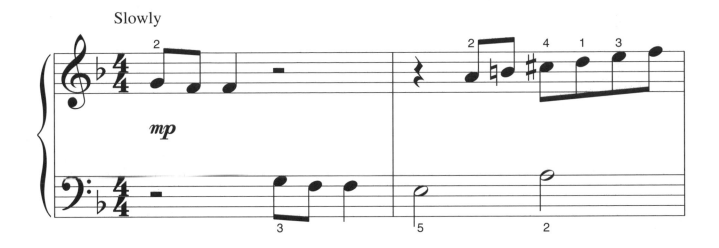

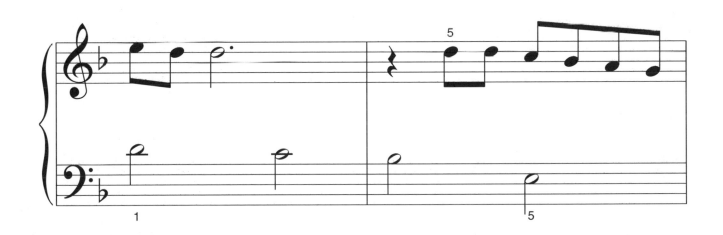

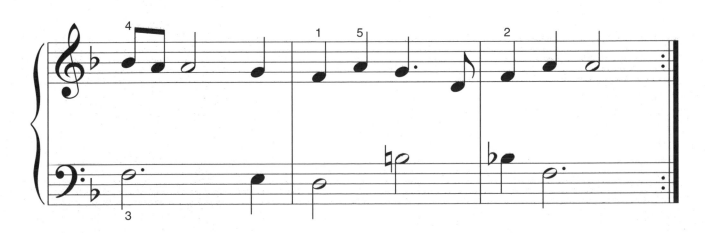

LOVE ME TENDER

Words and Music by ELVIS PRESLEY
and VERA MATSON

Flowing

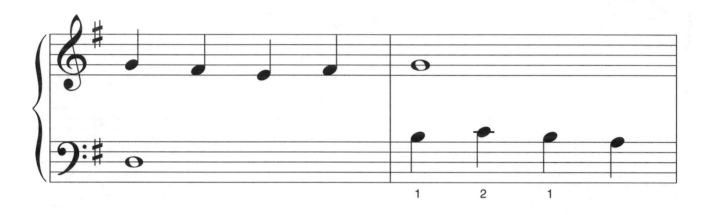

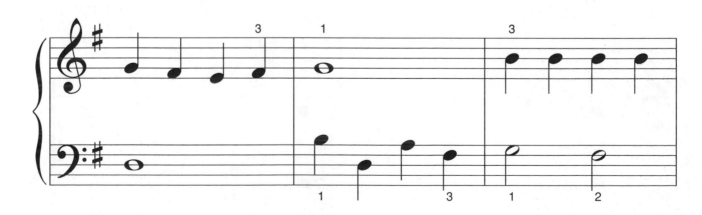

TEARS IN HEAVEN

Words and Music by ERIC CLAPTON
and WILL JENNINGS

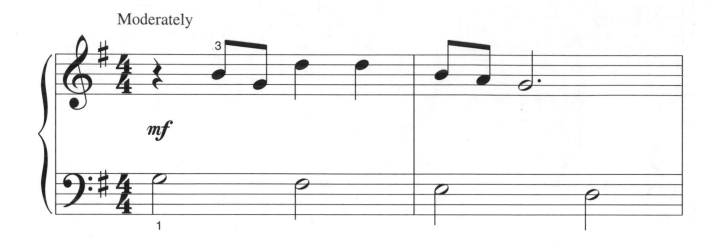

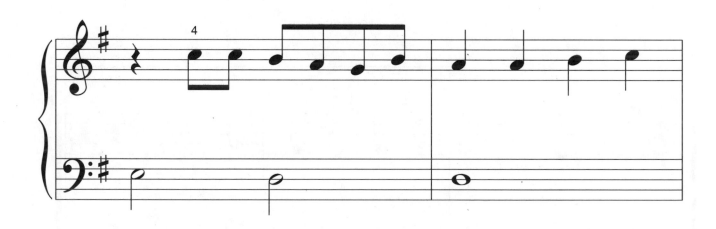

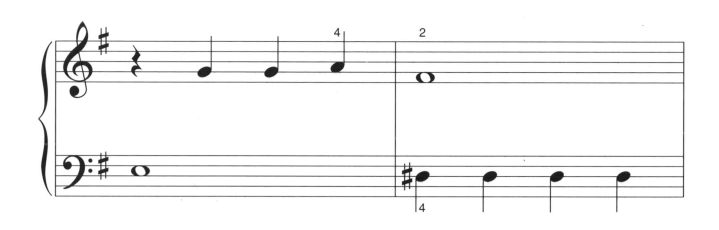

To Coda ⊕

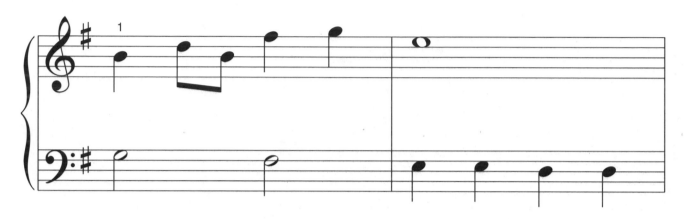

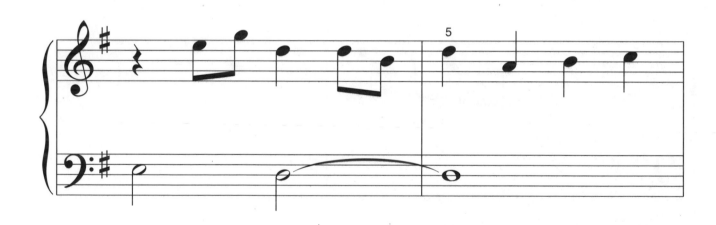

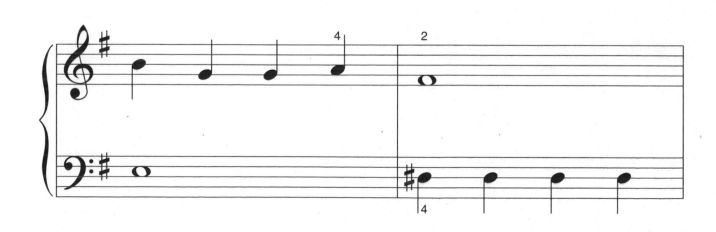

D.C. al Coda

CODA

Big Fun with Big-Note Piano Books!
These songbooks feature exciting easy arrangements for beginning piano students.

And Now It's Time for Silly Songs with Larry

10 songs, including: The Dance of the Cucumber • Endangered Love • The Hairbrush Song • His Cheeseburger • Lost Puppies • Love My Lips • The Pirates Who Don't Do Anything • The Song of the Cebú • The Water Buffalo Songs • The Yodeling Veterinarian of the Alps.
00310836 ....$12.95

Best Songs Ever

73 favorites, featuring: Body and Soul • Born Free • Crazy • Edelweiss • Fly Me to the Moon • Georgia on My Mind • Imagine • The Lady Is a Tramp • Memory • A String of Pearls • Tears in Heaven • Unforgettable • You Are So Beautiful • more.
00310425 ....$19.95

Broadway Favorites

Bill Boyd
12 Broadway favorites for big-note piano, including: All I Ask of You • Edelweiss • Everything's Coming Up Roses • I Dreamed a Dream • Sunrise, Sunset • and more!
00290184 ....$8.95

Children's Favorites Movie Songs

16 favorites from films, including: The Bare Necessities • Beauty and the Beast • Can You Feel the Love Tonight • Do-Re-Mi • Feed the Birds • The Lonely Goatherd • My Funny Friend and Me • Raiders March • The Rainbow Connection • So Long, Farewell • Tomorrow • Yellow Submarine • You'll Be in My Heart (Pop Version) • Zip-A-Dee-Doo-Dah.
00310838 ....$10.95

Children's Favorites

14 songs children love, including: The Brady Bunch • Casper the Friendly Ghost • Going to the Zoo • The Grouch Song • Hakuna Matata • The Name Game • The Siamese Cat Song • Winnie the Pooh • more.
00310282 ....$7.95

A Christmas Collection

33 simplified favorites, including: The Christmas Song (Chestnuts Roasting) • Frosty the Snow Man • A Holly Jolly Christmas • I Saw Mommy Kissing Santa Claus • Mister Santa • The Most Wonderful Day of the Year • Nuttin' for Christmas • Silver Bells • and more.
00221818 ....$10.95

Classical Music's Greatest Hits

24 beloved classical pieces including: Air on the G String • Ave Maria • By the Beautiful Blue Danube • Canon in D • Eine Kleine Nachtmusik • Für Elise • Ode to Joy • Romeo and Juliet • Waltz of the Flowers • more.
00310475 ....$9.95

Country Favorites

28 songs, including: Achy Breaky Heart • Down at the Twist & Shout • God Bless the U.S.A. • Your Cheatin' Heart • and more.
00222554 ....$10.95

Disney's Princess Collection

26 songs of love and hope, including: Belle • Can You Feel the Love Tonight • Colors of the Wind • Home • Kiss the Girl • Love • Part of Your World • Reflection • Some Day My Prince Will Come • Something There • A Whole New World • and more.
00316084 ....$14.95

Great Jazz Standards

arranged by Bill Boyd
20 songs, including: April in Paris • Don't Get Around Much Anymore • How High the Moon • It Don't Mean a Thing (If It Ain't Got That Swing) • When I Fall in Love • and more.
00222575 ....$12.95

God Bless America

15 patriotic songs, including Irving Berlin's classic title song and: America, the Beautiful • Battle Hymn of the Republic • A Mighty Fortress Is Our God • My Country, 'Tis of Thee (America) • O God, Our Help in Ages Past • The Star Spangled Banner • Stars and Stripes Forever • This Is My Country • This Land Is Your Land • We Shall Overcome • and more.
00310827 ....$9.95

Hymn Favorites

Includes 20 favorite hymns: Abide with Me • Blest Be the Tie That Binds • Jesus Loves Me • Nearer My God to Thee • Rock of Ages • What a Friend We Have in Jesus • and more.
00221802 ....$6.95

Les Misérables

14 songs, including: At the End of the Day • Bring Him Home • Castle On a Cloud • Do You Hear the People Sing • I Dreamed a Dream • In My Life • On My Own • and more.
00221812 ....$14.95

TV Hits

Over 20 theme songs that everyone knows, including: Brady Bunch • Cheers • (Meet) The Flintstones • Home Improvement • The Jetsons • Northern Exposure • Mr. Ed • The Munsters Theme • Won't You Be My Neighbor • and more fun favorites!
00221805 ....$9.95

Prices, contents, and availability subject to change without notice. Disney artwork © Disney Enterprises, Inc.

FOR MORE INFORMATION, SEE YOUR LOCAL MUSIC DEALER, OR WRITE TO:

HAL•LEONARD® CORPORATION
7777 W. BLUEMOUND RD. P.O. BOX 13819 MILWAUKEE, WI 53213

www.halleonard.com

0903

EASY PIANO
CD PLAY-ALONGS

Orchestrated Arrangements With You as the Soloist

This series lets you play along with great accompaniments to songs you know and love! Each book comes with a CD of complete professional performances and includes matching custom arrangements in Easy Piano format. With these books you can: Listen to complete professional performances of each of the songs; Play the Easy Piano arrangements along with the performances; Sing along with the recordings; Play the Easy Piano arrangements as solos, without the CD.

GREAT JAZZ STANDARDS
Volume 1
Easy Piano CD Play-Along
10 songs, including: Bewitched • Do Nothin' Till You Hear from Me • Don't Get Around Much Anymore • How Deep Is the Ocean (How High Is the Sky) • I'm Beginning to See the Light • It Might As Well Be Spring • My Funny Valentine • Satin Doll • Stardust • That Old Black Magic.
00310916 Easy Piano $14.95

FAVORITE CLASSICAL THEMES
Volume 2
Easy Piano CD Play-Along
This pack features 13 pieces: Bach: Air on the G String • Beethoven: Symphony No. 5, Excerpt • Bizet: Habanera • Franck: Panis Angelicus • Gounod: Ave Maria • Grieg: Morning • Handel: Hallelujah Chorus • Humperdinck: Evening Prayer • Mozart: Piano Concerto No. 21, Excerpt • Offenbach: Can Can • Pachelbel: Canon • Strauss: Emperor Waltz • Tchaikovsky: Waltz of the Flowers.
00310921 Easy Piano $14.95

BROADWAY FAVORITES
Volume 3
Easy Piano CD Play-Along
10 songs: All I Ask of You • Beauty and the Beast • Bring Him Home • Cabaret • Close Every Door • I've Never Been in Love Before • If I Loved You • Memory • My Favorite Things • Some Enchanted Evening.
00310915 Easy Piano $14.95

ADULT CONTEMPORARY HITS
Volume 4
Easy Piano CD Play-Along
10 songs including: Amazed • Angel • Breathe • I Don't Want to Wait • I Hope You Dance • I Will Remember You • I'll Be • It's Your Love • The Power of Love • You'll Be in My Heart (Pop Version).
00310919 Easy Piano $14.95

HIT POP/ROCK BALLADS
Volume 5
Easy Piano CD Play-Along
10 songs, including: Don't Let the Sun Go down on Me • From a Distance • I Can't Make You Love Me • I'll Be There • Imagine • In My Room • My Heart Will Go On (Love Theme from 'Titanic') • Rainy Days and Mondays • Total Eclipse of the Heart • A Whiter Shade of Pale.
00310917 Easy Piano $14.95

LOVE SONG FAVORITES
Volume 6
Easy Piano CD Play-Along
10 songs, including: Fields of Gold • I Honestly Love You • If • Lady in Red • More Than Words • Save the Best for Last • Three Times a Lady • Up Where We Belong • We've Only Just Begun • You Are So Beautiful.
00310918 Easy Piano $14.95

O HOLY NIGHT
Volume 7
Easy Piano CD Play-Along
15 holiday favorites, including: Deck the Hall • Go, Tell It on the Mountain • God Rest Ye Merry, Gentlemen • It Came upon the Midnight Clear • Jingle Bells • O Come, All Ye Faithful (Adeste Fideles) • O Holy Night • Silent Night • What Child Is This? and more.
00310920 Easy Piano $14.95

FOR MORE INFORMATION, SEE YOUR LOCAL MUSIC DEALER,
OR WRITE TO:

HAL•LEONARD®
CORPORATION
7777 W. BLUEMOUND RD. P.O. BOX 13819 MILWAUKEE, WI 53213

www.halleonard.com

Prices, contents, and availability subject to change without notice.